SENSE OF THE SACRED

Illuminated Book of Catholic Prayers

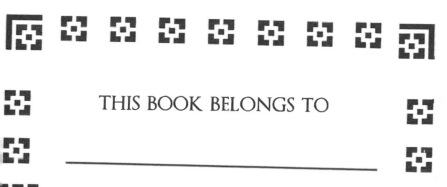

THIS BOOK BELONGS TO

_____

Nihil Obstat:
Rev. Timothy Hall
Censor Librorum
July 10, 2015

Imprimatur:
Most Rev. John Quinn
Bishop of Winona
July 10, 2015

24 23 22 21 20 19   2 3 4 5 6 7 8 9

ISBN: 978-1-68192-524-0 (Inventory No. T2413)
LCCN: 2019939971

Our Sunday Visitor Publishing Division
Our Sunday Visitor, Inc.
200 Noll Plaza
Huntington, IN 46750
1-800-348-2440
www.osv.com

Table of Contents

"When you sever the connection between
goodness and beauty, then goodness
is in danger of becoming abstract and merely
moral, and evil becomes fascinating."

Dietrich von Hildebrand

Finally, brethren, whatever is true,
whatever is honorable,
whatever is just,
whatever is pure,
whatever is lovely,
whatever is gracious,
if there is any excellence,
if there is anything worthy of praise,
think about these things.

Philippians 4:8 RSV

Renewal of Baptismal Vows

Almighty and Eternal God! You know all
things: You see the very bottom of my heart,
and You know that, however sinful I have
been till now, I am resolved, by the help of
your grace, to lie and serve you for the
remainder of my life.

And therefore, O my God, kneeling before the
throne of Your mercy, I renew, with all the
sincerity of my soul, the promises and vows
made for me in my baptism.

I renounce Satan with my whole heart, and
will henceforth have no connection with him.

I renounce all the pomps of Satan, that is, all
the vanities of the world, the false treaures of
its riches, honors and pleasures, and all its
corrupt teachings.

I renounce the works of Satan, that is, all
kinds of sins.

To You alone, O my God, I desire to cling;
Your word will I hear and obey; for you alone
I desire to live and to die.

Amen.

Prayer to the Sacred Heart of Jesus

most holy heart of Jesus, Fountain of every blessing,

I adore you, I love you, and with lively sorrow for my sins I offer you this poor heart of mine.

Make me humble, patient, pure and wholly obedient to your will. Grant, Good Jesus, that I may live in you and for you. Protect me in the midst of danger.

Comfort me in my afflictions. Give me health of body, assistance in my temporal needs, Your blessing on all that I do, and the grace of a holy death.

Amen.

Mary Help of Christians

ary Help of Christians, You listen with a Mother's love to all who look for your guidance.

I ask you to keep all those I love in your tender care.

Give me the strength to face up to life's difficulties and protect me from all spiritual and bodily harm.

Grant me an abundance of love so that I, too, may be a help to others, sharing with them in their time of need, and caring for them in their moments of distress.

Amen.

Mary Help of Christians, pray for us!

Prayer for Angelic Assistance

Lord Almighty, Creator of all life,

Thank You for creating the angels.

As dedicated and faithful servants, they instantly act upon Your commands.

Please direct Your angels to assist me, ensuring the accomplishment of Your work, in accordance with Your Divine will.

Always rekindle my mind to remember that Your angels are available to me as restrainers of diabolic obstacles.

Thank You Lord for Your auspice! Your kindness is infinitely good!

Amen.

Our Father

ur Father,
Who art in Heaven,
Hallowed be Thy Name,
Thy Kingdom come,
Thy Will be done
On Earth as it is in Heaven.

Give us this day
Our daily Bread,
And forgive us our trespasses,
As we forgive those
Who trespass against us,
And lead us not into temptation,
But deliver us from evil.

Amen.

Prayer Before an Image
of the Sacred Heart

Sacred Heart of Jesus,
Pour out Your benedictions
upon the Holy Church, upon its
priests, and upon all its
children.

Sustain the just, convert the
sinners, assist the dying,
deliver the souls in Purgatory,
and extend over all hearts the
sweet empire of Your love.

Amen.

Prayer to the Holy Cross

I adore You, O glorious Cross, which was adorned with the Heart and Body of my Savior Jesus Christ, stained and covered with blood.

I adore You, O Holy Cross, out of love for Him, Jesus, who is my Savior and my God.

Amen.

Hail, Holy Queen

ail, holy Queen, Mother of mercy, hail, our life, our sweetness and our hope. To thee do we cry, poor banished children of Eve: to thee do we send up our sighs, mourning and weeping in this vale of tears.

Turn then, most gracious Advocate, thine eyes of mercy toward us, and after this our exile, show unto us the blessed fruit of thy womb, Jesus,

O merciful, O loving, O sweet Virgin Mary!

Pray for us, oh holy Mother of God, that we may be made worthy of the promises of Christ.

Amen.

Prayer Before a Crucifix

ook down upon me, good and gentle Jesus, while before Thy face I humbly kneel and, with burning soul, pray and beseech Thee to fix deep in my heart lively sentiments of faith, hope and charity; true contrition for my sins, and a firm purpose of amendment while I contemplate with great love and tender pity, thy five most precious wounds, pondering over them within me and calling to mind the words which David, Thy prophet, said of You, my Jesus:

"They have pierced My hands and My feet, they have numbered all of My bones."

Amen.

Sanctus (Holy)

oly, holy, holy Lord,

God of power and might,

Heaven and earth are full
of Thy glory.

Hosanna in the highest.

Blessed is He who comes
 in the name of the Lord.

Hosanna in the highest!

The Blessed Sacrament

Sacrament Most Holy,

O Sacrament Divine,

All praise and all thanksgiving

Be every moment thine.

Amen.

The Memorare

Remember, O most gracious Virgin Mary, that never was it known that anyone who fled to thy protection, implored thy help, or sought thy intercession was left unaided.

Inspired by this confidence, I fly unto thee, o Virgin of virgins, my mother; to thee do I come, before thee I stand, sinful and sorrowful.

O Mother of the Word Incarnate, despise not my petitions, but in thy mercy hear and answer me.

Amen.

St Michael's Prayer

t. Michael the Archangel, defend us in the battle.

Be our safeguard against the wickedness and snares of the Devil.

May God rebuke him, we humbly pray, and do thou, O Prince of the heavenly hosts, by the divine power of God, cast into hell Satan, and all the evil spirits, who prowl about the world seeking the ruin of souls.

Amen.

Christ, King of the Universe

Christ Jesus, I acknowledge You as King of the Universe.

All that has been created has been made for You. Exercise upon me all Your rights. I renew my baptismal promises renouncing Satan and all his works and pomps.

I promise to lead a good Christian life and to do all in my power to procure the triumph of the rights of God and Your Church.

Divine Heart of Jesus, I offer You my poor actions in order to obtain that all hearts may acknowledge Your sacred royalty and that thus the reign of Your peace may be established throughout the universe.

Amen.

Children's Prayer to Mary

ear Mother of Jesus, look down upon me as I say my prayers slowly at my mother's knee.

I love thee, O Lady and please willest thou bring all little children to Jesus our King.

Amen.

Angelic Praises
of the Most Holy Trinity

Holy, holy, holy, Lord God of Hosts,

All the earth is full of Thy glory.

O Sacrament most Holy!

O Sacrament divine!

Be every moment Thine!

Amen.

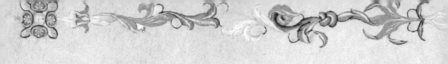

Prayer to Christ Crucified

Keep us in peace, O Christ our God, under the protection of Thy holy and venerable Cross: save us from enemies visible and invisible and account us worthy to glorify Thee with thanksgiving, together with the Father, and the Holy Ghost, now and forever, world without end.

Amen.

Our Lady of Walsingham

Mary, recall the solemn moment when Jesus, your divine son, dying on the cross, confided us to your maternal care.

You are our mother, we desire ever to remain your devout children. let us therefore feel the effects of your powerful intercession with Jesus Christ.

Make your name again glorious in the shrine once renowned throughout England by your visits, favors, and many miracles. Pray, O holy mother of God, for the conversion of England, restoration of the sick, consolation for the afflicted, repentance of sinners, peace to the departed.

O blessed Mary, mother of God, our Lady of Walsingham, intercede for us.

Amen.

Guardian Angel Prayer

ngel of God,

My guardian dear,

To whom God's love

Commits me here,

Ever this day, be at my side,

To light and guard,

To rule and guide.

Amen.

The Divine Praises

Blessed be God.

Blessed be His holy Name.

Blessed be Jesus Christ, true God and
true man.

Blessed be the Name of Jesus.

Blessed be His most Sacred Heart.

Blessed be His Precious Blood.

Blessed be Jesus in the Most Holy
Sacrament of the Altar.

Blessed be the Holy Spirit,
the Paraclete.

Blessed be the great Mother of God,
Mary most holy.

Blessed be her holy and
Immaculate Conception.

Blessed be her glorious assumption.

Blessed be the name of Mary,
Virgin and Mother.

Blessed be St. Joseph, her most chaste
spouse.

Blessed be God in His angels
and in His saints.

Glory Be

lory be to the Father,

And to the Son,

And to the Holy Spirit.

As it was in the beginning,

Is now, and ever shall be,

World without end.

Amen.

The Beatitudes

lessed are the poor in spirit; for theirs is the kingdom of heaven. Blessed are the meek; for they shall possess the land. Blessed are they that mourn; for they shall be comforted. Blessed are they that hunger and thirst after justice; for they shall be filled. Blessed are the merciful; for they shall obtain mercy. Blessed are the clean of heart; for they shall see God. Blessed are the peacemakers; for they shall be called the children of God. Blessed are they that suffer persecution for justice sake; for theirs is the kingdom of heaven. Amen.

Prayer to St Michael for Powerful Aid

lorious Prince of the heavenly hosts and victor over rebellious spirits, be mindful of me who am so weak and sinful and yet so prone to pride and ambition.

Lend me, I pray, thy powerful aid in every temptation and difficulty, and above all do not forsake me in my last struggle with the powers of evil.

Amen.

Easter Prayer

hrist is Risen: The world below lies desolate.

Christ is Risen: The spirits of evil are fallen.

Christ is Risen: The angels of God are rejoicing.

Christ is Risen: The tombs of the dead are empty.

Christ is Risen indeed from the dead, the first of the sleepers,

Glory and power are His forever and ever.

Amen.

Hail Mary

ail Mary, full of grace.

The Lord is with thee.

Blessed art thou among women,

And blessed is the fruit of thy womb, Jesus.

Holy Mary, Mother of God,

Pray for us sinners,

Now and at the hour of our death.

Amen.

Invocations in Honor
of the Holy Wounds

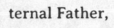

ternal Father,

I offer Thee the Wounds of Our
Lord Jesus Christ to heal the
wounds of our souls.

My Jesus,

Pardon and mercy through the
merits of Thy Sacred Wounds.

Amen.

Our Lady of Sorrows

 compassionate thee, O most sorrowful Mother! Thy heart was pierced with a sword of grief when Simeon foretold to thee in the Temple the ignominious death and the desolation of thy divine and most dear Son, which thou west destined one day to witness.

By the great anguish of thy suffering heart, O gracious Queen of the universe, impress upon my mind, in life and in death, the sacred Passion of Jesus and thine own sorrows.

Amen.

St Patrick's Breastplate

hrist with me,
Christ before me,
Christ behind me,
Christ in me,
Christ beneath me,
Christ above me,
Christ on my right,
Christ on my left,
Christ when I lie down,
Christ when I sit down,
Christ when I arise,
Christ in the heart of every man
who thinks of me,
Christ in the mouth of everyone
who speaks of me,
Christ in every eye that sees me,
Christ in every ear that hears me.
Amen.

The Cross Is

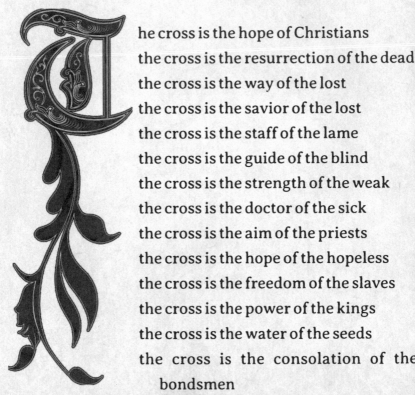

he cross is the hope of Christians

the cross is the resurrection of the dead

the cross is the way of the lost

the cross is the savior of the lost

the cross is the staff of the lame

the cross is the guide of the blind

the cross is the strength of the weak

the cross is the doctor of the sick

the cross is the aim of the priests

the cross is the hope of the hopeless

the cross is the freedom of the slaves

the cross is the power of the kings

the cross is the water of the seeds

the cross is the consolation of the bondsmen

the cross is the source of those who seek water

the cross is the cloth of the naked.

We thank you, Father, for the cross.

Amen.

Christit the King

Almighty, everlasting God,
Who in Thy beloved Son,
King of the whole world,
Hast willed to restore
 all things anew;
Grant in Thy Mercy
 that all the families
 of nations,
Rent asunder by
 the wound of sin,
May be subjected to
His most gentle rule,
Who with Thee lives
 and reigns
World without end.
 Amen.